MILESTONES IN
MODERN SCIENCE

The Discovery of DNA

Camilla de la Bédoyère

Gareth Stevens
Publishing

Please visit our web site at: www.garethstevens.com
For a free color catalog describing our list of high-quality books,
call 1-800-542-2595 (USA) or 1-800-387-3178 (Canada).
Our fax: (877) 542-2596.

Library of Congress Cataloging-in-Publication Data

De la Bédoyère, Camilla.
      The discovery of DNA/ by Camilla de la Bédoyère.
           p. cm. — (Milestones in modern science)
      Includes bibliographical references and index.
      ISBN 0-8368-5851-4 (lib. bdg.)
      1. DNA—History—Juvenile literature.   I. Title.   II. Series.
QP624.D123   2005
572.8'6'09—dc22   2005040470

This North American edition first published in 2006 by
World Almanac® Library
An imprint of Gareth Stevens Publishing
1 Reader's Digest Road
Pleasantville, NY 10570-7000 USA

This edition copyright © 2006 by World Almanac® Library. First published by Evans Brothers Limited. Copyright © 2005 by Evans Brothers Limited, 2A Portman Mansions, Chiltern Street, London W1U 6NR, United Kingdom. This U.S. edition published under license from Evans Brothers Limited.

Evans Brothers Consultant: Dr. Anne Whitehead
Evans Brothers Editor: Sonya Newland
Evans Brothers Designer: D. R. Ink, info@d-r-ink.com
Evans Brothers Picture researcher: Julia Bird

World Almanac® Library editor: Carol Ryback
World Almanac® Library cover design and art direction: Tammy West

Photo credits: (t) top, (b) bottom, (r) right, (l) left
Science Photo Library: /A. Barrington Brown cover, 5, 22(t); /Alfred Pasieka cover, 4(t), 20(t), 25(b), 26(l), 30; /Novosti 4(b); /Bluestone 6(t); /J.W. Shuler 6(b); /Tony Camacho 7; /A. Crump, TDR, WHO 8; /Damien Lovegrove 9(t); /Dr Gopal Murti 10(t), 27(b); /George Bernard 10(b); /Renee Lynn 11; /12, 13(b), 16, 19(b), 20(b), 22(b), 26(r); /Sinclair Stammers, prepared by Andy Cowap 13(t); /James King-Holmes 14; /J. De Mey, ISM 15(b); /T. H. Foto Verbung 18(t); /Eye of Science 18(b); /John Bavosi 24; /Ian Boddy 27(t); /Peter Menzel 28; /Andy Harmer 29(t); /ISM 31(b); /Astrid & Hanns-Frieder Michler 32(t); /David Parker 32(b); /J. C. Revy 33(b); / Hans-Ulrich Osterwalder 34(t); /Tom Myers 35(t); /Chris Knapton 35(b); /James King-Holmes 36(t);/P. H. Plailly/Eurelios 36(b); /Mark Clarke 37; /Simon Fraser/RVI, Newcastle-Upon-Tyne 38; /James King-Holmes 39; /Laguna Design 40; /BSIP, Laurent 41; /Lawrence Lawry 42(t); /Roger Harris 44. Science Society & Picture Library: /Science Museum 3, 23(b), 29(b), 42(b). CORBIS: /© Chris Collins 9(b); /© Archivo Iconografio, S.A. 31(t); / © Bettmann 33(t); /© Ted Streshinsky 34(b); /© Andrew Brookes 43.

Printed in the United States of America

2 3 4 5 6 7 8 9 10 09 08

CONTENTS

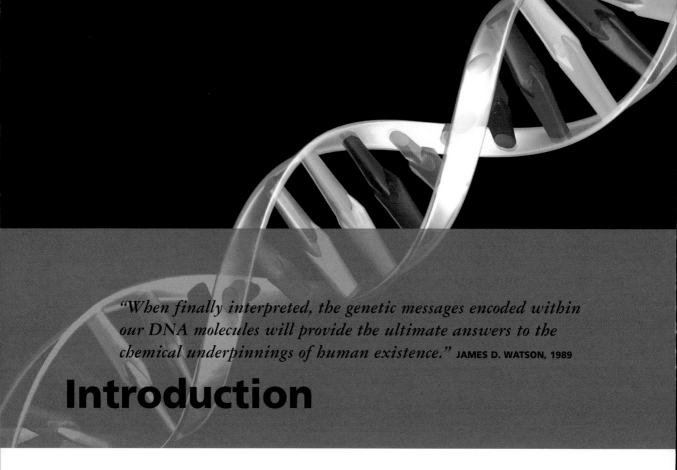

Introduction

Above: A computer graphic shows the twisted "double helix" (a twisted double spiral) shape of DNA—the molecule that carries information for inherited characteristics.

Below: These rabbits have been cloned—one is an exact copy of the other. Like identical twins, they share exactly the same genes. Cloning is just one example of genetic engineering, a science that evolved from the discovery of the structure of DNA.

In 1953, American James Watson and Englishman Francis Crick made one of the most important scientific discoveries of the twentieth century. They determined the structure of DNA—a large molecule found in nearly every cell of all organisms. DNA contains all the information required for life.

When scientists begin their quest for knowledge, they are often armed with little more than a good idea or a question that needs answering. The story of the discovery of DNA is similar to many in science. For centuries, people tried to unravel the mysteries of inheritance. Why do children look like their parents? How does the message of "likeness" get carried from parent to offspring? How does one cell replicate itself? With Watson's and Crick's discovery, scientists stood on the brink of answering some of these questions. But Watson and Crick are only two players in the fascinating story of DNA. Their achievement was the culmination of years of research by many other scientists without whom the mystery of genetic inheritance may have remained just that: a mystery.

Watson's and Crick's work heralded the beginning of a new era in which scientists could at last start to piece together the manner in which characteristics pass from one generation of organisms to another. The discovery of the structure of DNA, although significant, was only one of many steps toward genetic engineering and other exciting developments in science and medicine that now lie before us. It's a story of missed opportunities, blind alleys, and moments of pure genius.

Like many other scientific discoveries, Watson's and Crick's achievement carried with it enormous potential to change our world. It also brought us a new understanding of life on Earth. With this knowledge comes power, and with such power comes new questions—questions not always about the science itself, but how we can best use it. And, it poses moral and ethical questions that are often more difficult to unravel than the structure of DNA itself.

Below: A 1953 photograph shows James Watson (left) and Francis Crick (right) and a much larger-than-life model representing the structure of DNA—the "molecule of life."

CHAPTER ONE

"No one will ever be able to write a definitive history of how the structure {of DNA} was established. Nonetheless, I feel the story should be told." **JAMES D. WATSON, 1967**

DNA—The Stuff of Life

Above: *Familial similarities, such as hair color, eye color, or the shape of the nose, are determined by DNA, the molecule that passes characteristics from one generation to another.*

Below: *Human pancreatic cells magnified 3,200x. Pink indicates DNA; green and blue strands indicate the cell proteins.*

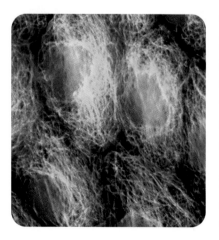

For years, the mystery of what controlled inherited features—in plants, animals, and humans—was investigated by scientists without much success, so the discovery of DNA marked a significant turning point in biological science. Today, we understand not only what makes each of us unique, but also how some characteristics are passed on to our offspring, while others are not. But what exactly is DNA? And how does it work?

WHAT IS DNA?

Living things are made up of cells and each cell (except mature red blood cells) contains DNA (deoxyribonucleic acid). DNA is the only molecule found in living things that makes copies of, or "replicates," itself. This is significant because new cells that form when a cell divides need their own DNA to grow and divide further.

Microscopic views of cells reveal paired strands of DNA, called chromosomes, coiled up within the nuclei. Most human cells have 23 pairs or 46 chromosomes each. If it were possible to unravel these miniscule strands, the DNA in a single cell would stretch for more than 6 feet (182 centimeters).

Cells use the DNA "instructions" to replicate themselves and to run and control all the chemical reactions that occur in every living thing. These DNA instructions, called genes, also contain codes for making cell proteins. These proteins enable cells to produce the chemicals necessary for cells to function. Much like living recipes, genes hold the keys for making each type of protein. The study of genes, and the way their information passes to the next generation, is called genetics.

HERE'S LOOKING AT YOU

Genetics involves looking at the similarities and differences between living things. Humans and chimpanzees are different creatures, yet their genes reveal that the two species are extremely similar—in fact, they share about 98.5 percent of their genetic code. People in the same family often share similar physical features, but each has a unique genetic code.

Fact

IMPORTANT PROTEINS

★ HEMOGLOBIN: the protein in blood that carries oxygen.

★ COLLAGEN: a fibrous protein that forms support structures, such as bones and skin.

★ MELANIN: a protective skin protein in human and animals that determines color.

★ ENZYMES: proteins found in all living cells that cause chemical reactions essential for life.

★ ANTIBODIES: proteins that protect the body against attack by bacteria and viruses.

Left: Chimpanzees are very different from humans in many respects, but share more than 98 percent of their DNA. Many scientists believe that this fact supports the idea that humans evolved from the same animal line as apes.

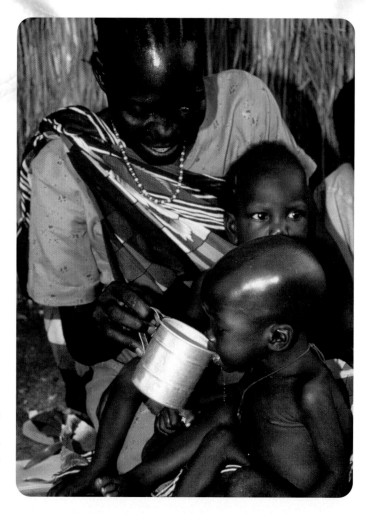

Right: *"Acquired variations" are caused by the environment rather than inheritance. Children in some areas of developing countries, therefore, might be smaller or more prone to illness not through any inherited characteristic, but because of their environment.*

DNA is not the sole governing factor for a child's development, however. Environmental factors often cause physical differences—known as "acquired" or "environmental" variations—even in children from the same family. For instance, a child who receives a diet high in the proper nutrients may grow to be much stronger and taller than his or her sibling who suffers stunted growth as a result of malnutrition. Other differences, caused by "inherited" variation, are the result of the genes a person inherited from his or her parents.

Some inherited variations, such as hair or eye color, are obvious. Others, such as blood group or a genetic condition such as sickle-cell anemia, are not. Blood tests determine these inherited variations. Every one of us has a unique genetic code, or master plan, which makes us different from everyone else. Environment can affect how that code is played out during our lives. The study of DNA and how it works may help scientists control and change some inherited features.

For thousands of years, farmers bred plants and animals with useful characteristics. Originally, long-stemmed wheat plants produced few grains of wheat.

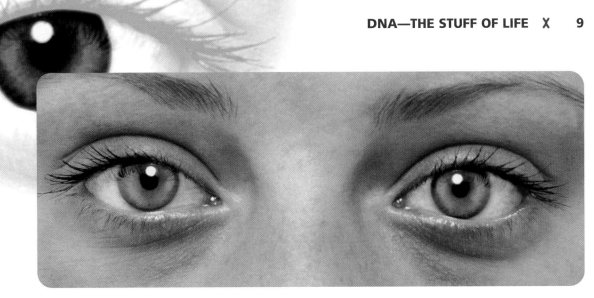

Farmers preferred plants with shorter stems and more grains and used those plants to pass the desired inherited variations from one generation to the next. When early farmers began selective breeding, they did not understand how characteristics passed between plants. The discovery of DNA revealed the mechanism for inherited variation. The route to that discovery followed a complex path.

Above: Eye color depends upon the genes inherited from both parents. Blue-eyed offspring occur when both parents carry the recessive gene for eye color.

Fact

DOG BREEDS

Selective breeding, sometimes known as "artificial breeding," is often practiced with living beings. Dog breeders choose particular characteristics, such as leg height, coat color, or even longevity, that they want to preserve in the breed. The breeders then mate dogs with those features in the hope of producing "perfect" offspring to sell for profit or to show in competitions.

Right: Selective breeding creates plants, crops, and even animals with certain characteristics that make them "better." Breeders developed the Doberman Pinscher breed through years of selectively mating several breeds of canines.

CHAPTER TWO

"It at once struck me that ... favorable variations will tend to be preserved, and unfavorable ones to be destroyed. The result of this would be the formation of new species." **CHARLES DARWIN, 1887**

Groundwork in Genetics

Above: *The X and Y chromosomes determine a person's sex. Nearly every cell in the human body contains forty-six chromosomes in its nucleus.*

Below: *Carl Linnaeus devised a plant classification system based on the number of male or female sex organs each had. The preface to his 1792 book on science and nature explains his classification system.*

PREFACE. v

The five subsequent Classes are distinguished not by the number of the males, or stamens, but by their union or adhesion, either by their anthers, or filaments, or to the female or pistil.

XVI. ONE BROTHERHOOD, *Monadelphia.* Many Stamens united by their filaments into one company; as in the second Figure below of No. xvi.

XVII. TWO BROTHERHOODS, *Diadelphia.* Many Stamens united by their filaments into two Companies; as in the uppermost Fig. No. xvii.

XVIII. MANY BROTHERHOODS, *Polyadelphia.* Many Stamens united by their filaments into three or more companies, as in No. xviii.

XIX. CONFEDERATE MALES, *Syngenefia.* Many Stamens united by their anthers; as in first and second Figures, No. xix.

XX. FEMININE MALES, *Gynandria.* Many Stamens attached to the pistil.

During the seventeenth and eighteenth centuries, an intellectual movement called the Enlightenment developed in Europe. During this period, new ideas regarding God, man, reason, and nature resulted in a revolution in art and science. People tested ideas using reason and deduction—a search for knowledge that continues today. Some scientists challenged the biblical view that God created all the animals and plants. The scientists began investigating the nature and origins of all life.

CLASSIFICATION AND EVOLUTIONARY CHARACTERISTICS

Carl Linnaeus (1707–1778) was a Swedish botanist. In 1735, he published *Systema Naturae* ("System of Nature"), in which he grouped animals and plants according to their shared characteristics. Creatures with cat-like features, for example, were grouped together in a process called taxonomy.

Linnaeus did not believe in evolution or extinction,

because if living things changed or died out, it meant that God's creations were not perfect. Linnaeus's system of classification did, however, establish a foundation for evolutionary science: the idea that genetically related organisms might share similar characteristics.

As the eighteenth century drew to a close, it became apparent to scientists that animals and plants could in fact change and develop over time. French botanist Jean Baptiste Lamarck (1744–1829) suggested the first detailed theory of how this might occur.

Lamarck called his theory "the inheritance of acquired characteristics." He hypothesized that body organs might develop through use or waste away through disuse. These changes would then be passed on to the animal's offspring. For instance, he believed that giraffes were originally similar in size and shape to the antelopes of the African plains. When food was in short supply, the ancestors of the giraffe stretched their necks to reach leaves high in the trees. In Lamarck's view, animals in which the stretching resulted in a longer neck survived, and their offspring inherited a longer neck.

Although scientists do not, generally, believe that Lamarck's theory of adaptation was correct, he was one of the first to accept the idea that such changes do occur and to suggest a way in which the changes come about.

SURVIVAL OF THE FITTEST

On December 27, 1831, the HMS *Beagle* set sail from England on a five-year journey around the globe. The ship's doctor was an English naturalist who was little-known at the time, but who is now heralded as one of the greatest scientists of all time: Charles Darwin (1809–1882).

In South America, Darwin found numerous fossils and noticed that life-forms appeared to have either changed ("evolved") or become extinct over time. When he landed on the tiny Pacific Ocean islands that

Fact

BINOMIAL CLASSIFICATION
Binomial means two names. Linnaeus's system for naming specific creatures involves using two Latin names—one for genus (the group), and one for species (the individual). Scientists from around the world use binomial classification to refer to a specific animal. For example, *Panthera leo* refers to a lion. *Panthera* indicates that the animal belongs to the large cat group (defined by their ability to roar) and *leo* indicates the species.

Above: Lions belong to the big-cat genus—specified by the first part of their Latin name, Panthera. *Jaguars, leopards, and tigers also belong to the genus* Panthera.

1

2

3

4

Above: *Sketches of the finches Darwin saw in the Galápagos Islands. He suggested that living creatures evolved to adapt to the food supplies available in their habitats. Finches with large, strong beaks (1 and 2) ate seeds, while those with shorter, sharper beaks (3 and 4) ate insects.*

form the Galápagos archipelago, about 600 miles (1,000 kilometers) off the coast of Ecuador, he encountered many varied and unique animals. These creatures inspired him to develop his theory of evolution.

Darwin discovered thirteen finch species living on the hundreds of islands. He noticed that, although the species of these birds were very similar, they had small differences that made them well suited to their particular habitat and main food supply.

These birds were not found anywhere else in the world—just on the Galápagos Islands. This fact made Darwin wonder whether the finches had all descended from just one pair of finches that had slowly adapted and evolved to fit the different habitats found on the islands.

Years after Charles Darwin returned to England, he was still thinking about the information he had collected during his voyage and what it could mean. He read a book, entitled *An Essay on the Principle of Population*, in which its author, Thomas Malthus (1766–1834), argued that populations of animals or humans can grow too large for their available food sources and therefore compete with others of the same species to survive: the strongest would live, the weakest would die.

Darwin had an idea: What if evolution happens in a similar way? If animals compete for a food source or a habitat, successful individuals could mate and pass their successful characteristics on to their offspring. This "natural selection" of the strongest would lead to the "survival of the fittest," a phrase which means "best suited to the environment," and not—as some people later interpreted it—"the strongest or best." Although Darwin explained how variations and inherited characteristics contributed to his theory of evolution, he could not explain exactly *how* the characteristics passed from one generation to another. Another scientist, Gregor Mendel (1822–1884), made the next great step forward.

Fact

DARWIN'S INSPIRATION

When Charles Darwin sailed on the HMS *Beagle*, he took with him the first volume of Charles Lyell's (1797-1875) book, *Principles of Geology*. In it, Lyell suggested that Earth was 240 million years old. At the time, analysis of Bible stories led many people to believe Earth was only six thousand years old. This made a huge difference when considering how long living things took to evolve, and it backed up the evidence for Lyell's theory that Darwin found in the landscapes, rocks, and fossils throughout his journey.

Right: These ammonites are fossils of extinct ocean animals that lived between 380 and 65 million years ago. The discovery of fossils like these proved that Earth had existed for much longer than people in Darwin's time generally believed.

Key People

Alfred Russel Wallace (1823–1913) was, like Darwin, a British naturalist. In 1858, he sent Darwin a copy of his essay that contained a theory of evolution remarkably similar to the one Darwin had been formulating. Wallace had also been influenced by Lyell's book. Wallace coined the phrase "survival of the fittest." Wallace and Darwin jointly presented their ideas on natural selection to the Linnaean Society. Although both men came separately to similar conclusions, Darwin's name is the one forever linked with the evolutionary theory of "survival of the fittest."

PARTICLES OF INHERITANCE

The mysteries of inheritance fascinated many scientists in the middle of the nineteenth century. In 1856, Austrian monk Gregor Mendel began a series of experiments in the garden of his monastery. Mendel knew that the garden pea plant had a variety of inherited characteristics, such as flower color and plant height. He wanted to investigate how these characteristics were passed from one generation to the next.

Mendel took pollen from tall pea plants and used it to fertilize short pea plants, which then grew seeds. When Mendel planted these seeds, he may have expected the new plants to show a blend of their parents' characteristics and all be of medium height or of a mixture of small and tall. In fact, all the hybrid plants were tall. He took each hybrid,

Right: Monk and botanist Gregor Mendel conducted breeding experiments with pea plants. He discovered that certain "laws of heredity" governed some aspects of offspring.

Fact

DEFINITIONS

★ DOMINANT PARTICLES: particles of inheritance that determine a character- istic, even when only one of those particles is present in the offspring.

★ RECESSIVE PARTICLES: particles of inheri- tance that only appear if the dominant version is not present.

★ HYBRID: offspring that result from the cross-breeding of two varieties within the same species.

★ POLLINATION: the transfer of pollen from one plant to another.

★ SELF-POLLINATION: the fertilization of a plant using its own pollen.

★ SEX CELLS: cells in pollen that allow plants to breed. Sex cells (also called germ cells or gametes) have half the normal number of chromosomes.

self-pollinated it, and raised the seeds that came from these plants. Three-fourths of those new plants were tall and one quarter were short—a ratio of 3:1.

Each time Mendel repeated his experiments, he got the same results: The first set, or generation, of offspring shared the same characteristics. When he self-pollinated the first generation, the second generation produced mixed characteristics, but no blending of traits occurred.

Mendel believed that "particles of inheritance" passed from parents to offspring. He suggested that each parent passed on one particle to its offspring, and that some factors, such as "tall," were dominant to others, such as "short." A plant with one "tall factor" and one "short" factor would be tall. Mendel called the weaker factors "recessive," and said that two recessive factors were required to make the characteristic appear in the offspring.

Unfortunately, Mendel's extraordinary contribution to science was largely ignored until 1900, sixteen years after his death. His particles of inheritance were what we now call genes. Gregor Mendel is regarded as the "Father of Genetics."

MENDEL'S PEA EXPERIMENT

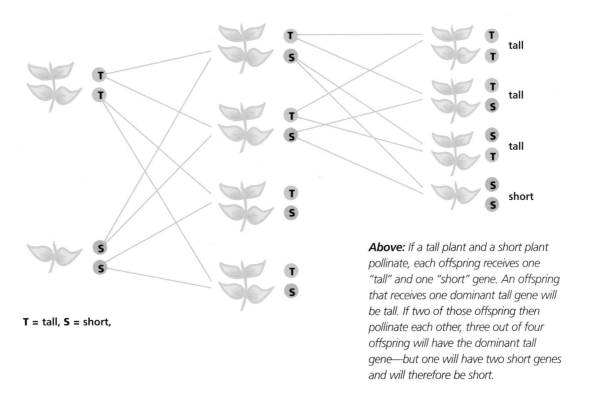

tall

tall

tall

short

T = tall, **S** = short,

Above: If a tall plant and a short plant pollinate, each offspring receives one "tall" and one "short" gene. An offspring that receives one dominant tall gene will be tall. If two of those offspring then pollinate each other, three out of four offspring will have the dominant tall gene—but one will have two short genes and will therefore be short.

WHAT HAPPENS INSIDE A CELL?

At the time Darwin and Mendel were working on their theories of inheritance, relatively little was known about cells, the building blocks of all living organisms. The nucleus of a cell was identified and named by Scottish botanist Robert Brown (1773–1858) in 1831, but it was another ten years before a dividing cell was observed under a microscope and the process described.

By the late nineteenth century, microscopes were powerful enough to reveal tiny shapes appearing in the nucleus of a cell before it divided. German biologist Walther Flemming (1843–1905) was intrigued by these and conducted experiments to find out what they were. He added artificial dyes to his cell samples and found that the little pieces of matter inside the nuclei took up the dye particularly strongly. He called this material "chromatin," from the Greek word for

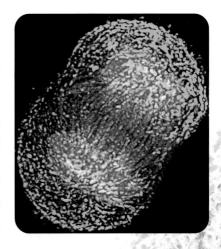

Above: By the late nineteenth century, more powerful microscopes were available. They allowed scientists to learn more about what happens inside cells and how they divide. Cell division is called mitosis (see p. 17).

"color." When the cell divided, the chromatin formed strands, or threads. These strands were later named chromosomes.

In the 1880s, two more important steps were taken toward the discovery of DNA. Scientists learned that each cell in an organism has the same number of chromosomes, and that this number is the same for all members of a particular species. Humans, for example, have 46 chromosomes. Chimpanzees and potatoes have 48. August Weismann (1834–1914), a German biologist, made a new suggestion: Perhaps the chromosomes passed on the information that developed into inherited characteristics. Weismann realized that if each sex cell, such as a human sperm and egg, had the normal number of chromosomes (46), then fertilization should cause the offspring to have double that number (92). Instead, Weismann suggested that the sex cells actually had half the number of chromosomes. This was later proved true: Sex cells are the only cells in the human body that contain only 23 chromosomes. When a sperm fertilizes an egg, the combined number once again equals 46 chromosomes—the correct number for humans.

FURTHER RESEARCH ON GENES

In 1900, Dutch botanist Hugo de Vries (1848–1935) was studying Darwin's theory of inheritance when he noticed a flaw: Natural selection alone does not adequately explain variations between individuals. De Vries suggested that each characteristic was carried on a separate unit, which he called a "pangene." Before publishing his theory, however, de Vries discovered that Gregor Mendel, who had worked on the same problem thirty-five years previously, had already identified these discrete units of inheritance.

De Vries tested Mendel's findings and, in doing so, took the research further. He was breeding evening primrose flowers and discovered that, every now and then, a new flower color was produced in a pure line. This was then passed on to future generations. He called these random changes "mutations." De Vries brought Mendel's work into the limelight: The

Key People

Johann Friedrich Miescher (1844–95) was a Swiss biochemist. He used the latest technology in microscopes to study cell nuclei. Miescher discovered that the nucleus of each cell contained an unknown substance, which he called "nucleic acid." He noticed that proteins were found near nucleic acids and wondered whether proteins or nucleic acids might have something to do with inheritance. His contemporaries thought that the proteins were most likely to fulfill this role. The nucleic acid Miescher identified was actually DNA—but the significance of his discovery was not realized until many years later.

Fact

MITOSIS AND MEIOSIS

Mitosis is the method by which most cells divide. The threads of chromatin replicate themselves and form chromosomes. The membrane around the nucleus breaks down and "spindles" appear in the cell. These spindles pull apart the chromosomes so that two sets of "daughter" chromosomes are formed. After this, the nuclei membrane reforms, producing two new cells with identical genetic properties. Meiosis is the cell division method that produces sex cells. It is similar to mitosis, but in the final stage of meiotic cell division, each daughter cell contains half the number of total chromosomes for that organism.

MITOSIS
Cells replicate (copy) themselves

MEIOSIS
DNA replicates itself to produce sex cells

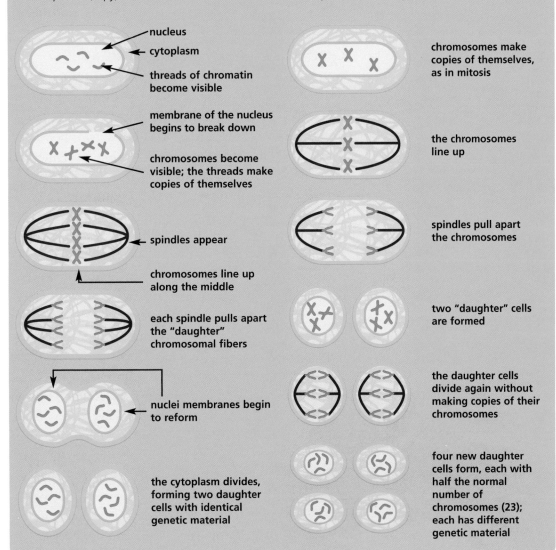

MITOSIS

nucleus

cytoplasm

threads of chromatin become visible

membrane of the nucleus begins to break down

chromosomes become visible; the threads make copies of themselves

spindles appear

chromosomes line up along the middle

each spindle pulls apart the "daughter" chromosomal fibers

nuclei membranes begin to reform

the cytoplasm divides, forming two daughter cells with identical genetic material

MEIOSIS

chromosomes make copies of themselves, as in mitosis

the chromosomes line up

spindles pull apart the chromosomes

two "daughter" cells are formed

the daughter cells divide again without making copies of their chromosomes

four new daughter cells form, each with half the normal number of chromosomes (23); each has different genetic material

Above: In the early twentieth century, scientists discovered that Mendel's laws of heredity were not as straightforward as they seemed. Some plants, such the evening primrose, sometimes mutated. They produced a different color flower even when the parent plants were of the same type.

Below: The fruit fly, Drosophila melanogaster, *has been used in genetic research since the beginning of the twentieth century. It has a short life span and reproduces very rapidly, so the results of experiments can be seen without having to wait a long time for offspring.*

science of genetics was about to take a great leap forward.

The transmission of characteristics is not always simple. English biologist William Bateson (1861–1926) learned that, in some instances, two genes are always linked. By breeding sweet peas, Bateson discovered a link between flower color and pollen shape: Long pollen produced purple flowers and round pollen produced red flowers.

"Such a word is badly wanted and if it were desirable to coin one, Genetics might do."
WILLIAM BATESON, 1905

CHROMOSOMES—THE GENE CARRIERS

By the beginning of the twentieth century, scientists realized that chromosomes might be the part of the cell that carried the genetic information. They began to search for the "pangenes," the units of inheritance. Thomas Hunt Morgan (1866–1945), an American geneticist, chose to study the fruit fly, *Drosophila melanogaster*, because they breed very quickly.

Many inherited differences soon appeared in *Drosophila* as a result of mutation. Morgan discovered that most mutations happened just as Mendel's work predicted—some were dominant and some were recessive. Certain characteristics, however, such as eye color, depended upon the sex cell each parent contributed to the offspring. Morgan knew that in the human body, male and female sex chromosomes differ slightly: Females have two X chromosomes, while males have one X and one Y. He suggested that the gene that determined eye color for the fruit flies was carried on the X chromosome—and he was eventually able to prove this. In 1933, Morgan received the Nobel Prize in physiology or medicine for his enormous contribution to genetics.

Fact

X AND Y CHROMOSOMES

Humans have 23 pairs of chromosomes in each cell. Twenty-two of the chromosomal pairs are autosomes—not sex chromosomes. The twenty-third pair has two sex chromosomes—one each from the mother and father. Sex chromosomes resemble letters of the alphabet. A female can only transfer an "X" chromosome to offspring; the father can transfer either an "X" or a "Y" chromosome. The twenty-third chromosomal pair of the resulting baby is either "XX" (a girl) or "XY" (a boy).

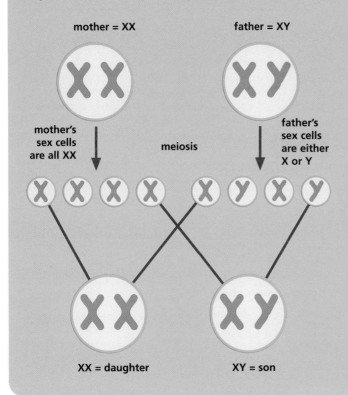

Left: A person's sex depends on the sex chromosomes inherited from the parents. Females contribute only X chromosomes, but males contribute either X or Y chromosomes. An X inherited from both the mother and father produces a daughter; an X from the mother and a Y from the father produces a son.

Key People

Archibald Garrod (1857–1936), an English doctor working in the early twentieth century, studied four hereditary diseases caused by deficiencies in certain enzymes (proteins that enable chemical reactions to occur within the body). He called them "inborn errors of metabolism" and suggested the "one gene, one enzyme" hypothesis. According to this theory, one gene makes one enzyme, and a genetic mutation could prevent the production of that enzyme, causing a hereditary disease. He was later proved correct.

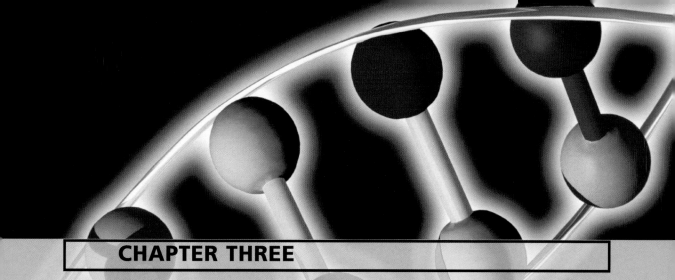

CHAPTER THREE

"We wish to suggest a structure for the salt of deoxyribonucleic acid, DNA. This structure has novel features which are of considerable biological interest."

WATSON AND CRICK, FROM THEIR ARTICLE IN THE SCIENTIFIC JOURNAL *NATURE*, 1953

DNA Revealed

Above: *DNA bases pair up in a specific manner. Guanine (orange) pairs with cytosine (green), and adenine (blue) pairs with thymine (red). The sequence in which these pairs appear creates a genetic code.*

Below: *Phoebus Levene discovered the important molecule ribonucleic acid in the nucleus of cells.*

By the early twentieth century, scientists knew that chromosomes carried genes—the units that passed characteristics to offspring—but no one knew why the genes performed this function. For the next several decades, scientists searched for the answer.

NUCLEIC ACIDS: DNA AND RNA

Researchers were aware of the nucleic acids in cell nuclei as far back as the 1870s. When Johann Friedrich Miescher discovered them, though, no one realized their significance. Thirty years later, a Russian-born scientist, Phoebus Levene (1869–1940), studying nucleic acids in the United States, discovered that one of them contained a type of sugar, ribose. He named the molecule ribonucleic acid, or RNA. He also isolated nucleotides, the chain-like structures that form the basis of nucleic acid molecules. Twenty years later, Levene discovered the structure of a second nucleic acid, deoxyribonucleic acid (DNA), which contains the sugar, deoxyribose.

Levene demonstrated that DNA is a chain of millions of nucleotides linked together, and that each nucleotide consists of three parts: deoxyribose (a sugar), a phosphate group, and a nitrogenous base. Four different types of nitrogenous bases—adenine (A), thymine (T), cytosine (C), and guanine (G)—are repeated over and over again. Levene suspected that DNA might play a part in carrying hereditary information, but for many years scientists dismissed the notion that a simple, four-base molecule could perform this complicated role.

In 1944, Levene's suggestions were proved correct. The Canadian bacteriologist Oswald Avery (1877–1955) managed to pass genetic information from dead bacteria to live bacteria. He realized that the DNA carried that information.

Although DNA had been revealed as the molecule of life, no one really knew how it worked. Until scientists could understand its structure, they could not hope to comprehend how the genes replicated themselves and passed on information. In 1950, Edwin Chargaff (1905–2002) and his team used a technique called chromatography to show that the four bases of nucleotides were always found in very strict ratios: The numbers of adenine and thymine groups are always equal, as are the numbers of cytosine and guanine groups. This is called "Chargaff's rule," and its importance became clear within a few years.

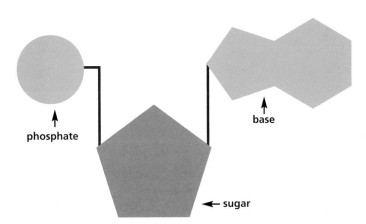

Left: *Nucleotides are the "links" in the DNA chain. Each nucleotide is made up of a phosphate, a sugar, and one of four bases—A, G, C, and T. Millions of nucleotides link together to form DNA.*

phosphate

base

sugar

"There were scientists who thought that the evidence favoring DNA was inconclusive and preferred to believe that genes were protein molecules. . . . In contrast to popular conception, a goodly number of scientists are not only narrow-minded and dull, but also just stupid." **JAMES D. WATSON, 1967**

THE STRUCTURE OF DNA REVEALED

During the late 1940s and early 1950s, laboratories buzzed as scientists around the world raced to discover the structure of DNA. In England, Maurice Wilkins (1916–2004) worked with his colleague, Rosalind Franklin (1920–1958). Together, they took X-ray photographs of DNA crystals.

Background: *James Watson (right) and Francis Crick (left), photographed at the Cavendish Laboratory, in Cambridge, England, in 1953.*

Inset: *Rosalind Franklin took this revealing X-ray photograph of DNA crystals in 1953. X-rays bounce off the atoms inside the DNA molecule. As they leave the molecule, the rays form a pattern on photographic paper.*

Fact

TYPES OF MOLECULE

★ DEOXYRIBOSE: a sugar molecule that forms part of DNA. It is a pentose sugar, which means it has five carbon atoms.
★ NITROGENOUS BASES: adenine (A), guanine (G), cytosine (C), and thymine (T)—four types of ring-shaped molecules containing nitrogen and found in DNA.
★ PHOSPHATE GROUP: a molecule containing phosphate that helps form the "backbone" of the DNA molecule.
★ RIBOSE: a sugar molecule found in RNA. It is also a pentose sugar with five carbon atoms.

At the Cavendish Laboratory at Cambridge University, England, another two scientists, American James Watson (b. 1928), and Englishman Francis Crick (1916–2004), joined Wilkins in the quest. Although initially they were both working on other research, the mystery of DNA fascinated them and the two decided to work together to unravel it.

Meanwhile, British researcher Rosalind Franklin had produced the best photographic images of DNA then available. She knew that other scientists hoped to use

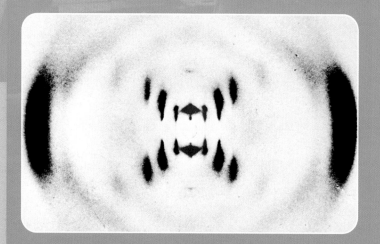

her research to develop their own theories about the structure of DNA. Franklin refused to share her findings with others because she feared that they would not give her proper credit for her work. Unfortunately, that is exactly what happened. In January 1953, Wilkins showed Watson and Crick the images he and Franklin had made. The men soon realized that only one molecular structure—a double helix (it resembles a spiral staircase)—could explain the images.

Watson, Crick, and Wilkins began building a model of the structure of DNA. At first, they used pieces of cardboard to determine how the bases fit together. They ended up with a structure best described as a double helix, which looks a somewhat like a twisting ladder. Sugar and phosphate blocks form the two long sides of the ladder, while paired nitrogenous bases—adenine with thymine and guanine with cytosine—form the rungs.

In 1962, Watson, Crick, and Wilkins received the Nobel Prize for physiology or medicine. Rosalind Franklin never shared their success. She died in 1958 at the age of thirty-seven. But her work, and that of many other scientists, contributed many pieces to a complex puzzle. Watson and Crick used those pieces and, with a mixture of inspiration, determination, and luck, unlocked the secret of the molecule of life.

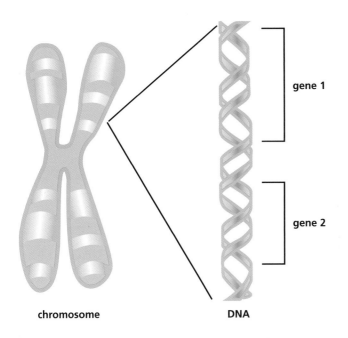

gene 1

gene 2

chromosome   DNA

Above: DNA is found on chromosomes. It is divided into sections called genes, which can vary in length along a stretch of DNA. Each gene controls an inherited characteristic.

Fact

X-RAY CRYSTALLOGRAPHY
A molecule's shape and structure provides insight into how it works. X-ray crystallography helps determine the 3-D structure of complex molecules that form crystals. As X-rays pass through a crystal, the unique shape diffracts, or bends, the beams according to the crystal's composition. Measurements of the degree to which the crystal causes diffraction of the X-rays produce an image of that crystal's molecular structure. X-ray crystallography thus reveals structures of proteins, hormones, nucleic acids, and vitamins.

Key People

Linus Pauling (1901–1994) was an American chemist who used X-ray diffraction and other techniques to calculate distances and angles between chemical bonds in molecules. He won the 1954 Nobel Prize in chemistry for determining the shape of proteins. Although he was later proved wrong by Watson and Crick, Pauling also suggested a structure for DNA. Instead of paper-and-pencil methods, Pauling constructed large-scale models of molecules. This method inspired Watson and Crick to follow suit.

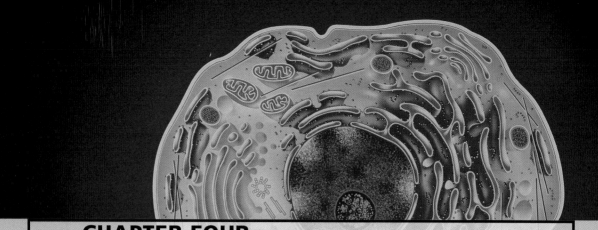

CHAPTER FOUR

"Our 46 chromosome 'threads' linked together would measure more than six feet. Yet the nucleus that contains them is less than four ten-thousandths of an inch in diameter."

RICK GORE, *NATIONAL GEOGRAPHIC*, 1976

Unraveling the Helix

Above: *A typical cell. The pink sphere in the middle is the nucleus, and the nucleolus (brown) contains the DNA. In the cytoplasm, the orange circles— the ribosomes—contain the RNA that helps produce proteins.*

Fact

PROTEINS

Protein production occurs constantly in the cytoplasm of cells. DNA, found in the nucleus, holds the codes for proteins. Free RNA in the nucleus copies the DNA protein code and transports it into the cytoplasm in the form of messenger RNA (mRNA). Each mRNA molecule contains the code for an amino acid, the building blocks of proteins.

Discovering the structure of DNA was important because it meant that scientists could start to determine how this relatively simple molecule conveys information. Watson and Crick suggested that if the two sugar-phosphate "backbones" of a DNA molecule separated, each of the strands could replicate, forming two complete copies of the original strand.

DNA CODES FOR PROTEINS

Watson and Crick suggested that DNA could also provide codes for making cell proteins. Because DNA is found inside the nucleus of a cell, but a cell's cytoplasm manufactures proteins, the scientists looked for a "messenger" molecule capable of carrying information from the DNA to the site of protein synthesis. This messenger molecule was ribonucleic acid (RNA)—the nucleic acid that Phoebus Levene had identified many years earlier (*see* p. 20).

RNA resembles DNA, but with only one strand instead of two. Like DNA, it has four different nitrogenous bases, but with uracil instead of thymine. DNA "unzips" to expose its bases and provide the code to create a particular protein. RNA nucleotides floating free in the nucleus join up with the exposed DNA bases to make copies. This process is similar to DNA replication, except that the RNA pairs uracil, rather than thymine, with adenine. The newly created RNA molecule, called messenger RNA (mRNA), then moves from the nucleus into the cytoplasm.

Inside the cytoplasm, the mRNA attaches to a ribosome. The ribosome "reads" the code contained on the mRNA and uses another RNA molecule, called transfer RNA (tRNA), to create the protein.

Different cells have different functions, and different parts of the DNA in any one cell may unzip at any time. Each cell needs different proteins for its specific type, and our bodies constantly create millions of proteins. Research on other organisms reveals that the genetic code is remarkably similar for all living things, from bacteria to humans. In fact, we share 30 percent of our DNA with a banana!

MUTATIONS IN THE GENETIC CODE

In the very early 1900s, Hugo de Vries proved that random changes occur in the phenotype (the appearance of an organism) of evening primrose flowers; he called these changes "mutations." Later,

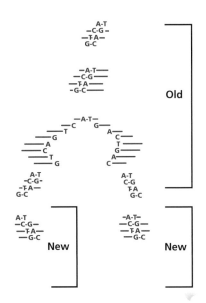

Above: *This diagram shows a DNA molecule separating to form two new molecules. Each strand of the original molecule acts as a template for the new one. Enzymes cause the separation of the two strands. The process of base pairing forms two new strands that are identical to the original strand—and to each other.*

Left: *Recent research shows that DNA is much more complex than first thought. Although tightly coiled, the double helix regularly changes into new shapes, sometimes weaving itself into knots. Scientists suspect that the constant jiggling and twisting of the DNA plays an important part in switching genes on and off. The sugar-phosphate backbone is shown in yellow; bases appear blue.*

Fact

GENES AND A NEW LIFE

A gene on a chromosome holds the code that passes hereditary information between generations. A gene can simply dictate the color of a flower, or it can help determine the sex of a human being. Genes on the 23 chromosomes in a human male sex cell (sperm) combine with the genes on the 23 chromosomes in a female sex cell (ovum) during fertilization. In this way, genetic material passes from one generation to the next. After millions of cell divisions, a new person is born. The baby's 46 chromosomes—half from from the father and half from the mother—contain a unique genotype (set of genes).

Above: *A complete set of human male chromosomes. Each of the 23 pairs contains one chromosome from each parent, for a total of 46 chromosomes. Males differ from females only in the last pair. Here, on the bottom right, an X- and Y-shaped chromosome comprise the 23rd pair. Genes on the Y chromosome hold the codes for the development of male features.*

researchers found that there were various ways of causing these mutations. In the 1930s, an American geneticist, Hermann Muller (1890–1967), showed that a blast of X-rays caused fruit flies to develop 150 times as many mutations as expected.

Watson and Crick used X-rays to induce mutations in bacteriophages—viruses that attack bacteria and

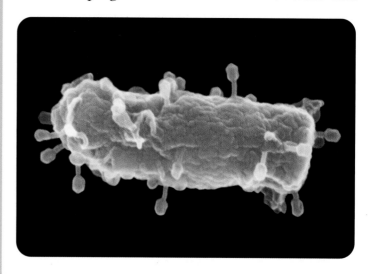

Above: *Bacteriophages are a type of virus; they are seen here as the brownish hexagonal shapes attacking a bacterium cell. Watson and Crick used bacteriophages to cause changes in a chromosome.*

instruct them to make more copies of the virus. The scientists found they could create mutations in a specific area on a chromosome and that the mutation changed the order of the nitrogenous bases A, T, G, and C.

In some cases, the chemical used to create the mutation became incorporated into the code. In other cases, the mutation eliminated a single base or part of the code. An incorrect code cannot properly instruct a cell to create a particular protein. Since proteins are essential for the life and function of every cell, errors in protein creation cause significant consequences.

Although scientists purposely created these mutations, or "mistakes," in the genetic code, mutations also happen naturally all the time.

MUTATIONS AND EVOLUTION

Charles Darwin's theory of evolution by natural selection relied on organisms producing changes in their phenotypes. These changes, or variations, gave them an advantage that enabled a particular animal to survive when another might die. Animals that survived could breed and therefore pass these variations on to the next generation. Genetic mutations cause this natural selection to take place.

Small changes, or mutations, sometimes occur in genes during the process of meiosis, when sex cells are produced (*see* p. 15). Mutations can prevent a fertilized egg from developing. Occasionally a mutation, such as a differently shaped beak or claw, does not prevent an embryo's development; it might even prove useful. In a competition for limited resources, such as food or mates, some of these changes often prove very helpful. Over millions of years, these accidental chromosomal variations became the driving force of evolution.

ABOVE: *A fertilized egg that splits in half produces two embryos with identical genes: Identical twins.*

Fact

SICKLE-CELL ANEMIA

Sickle-cell anemia (SSA) is an inherited and debilitating disease common in rural Africa, but it is also found in other parts of the world. In North America, about one in four hundred African Americans has SSA. The protein hemoglobin in red blood cells (RBCs) allows blood to carry oxygen around the body. Normal RBCs are round and flexible. In people affected with SSA, abnormal hemoglobin distorts the shape of the RBCs and makes them rigid. These abnormal RBCs can block blood flow around the body. The theory of natural selection suggests that people with sickle-cell anemia—who suffer and sometimes die from this disease—would be less likely to have children, and the disease would disappear over time. Research, however, shows that SSA also gives those who carry it a distinct advantage: They are less likely to develop malaria, a mosquito-borne disease that kills 2.5 million people every year.

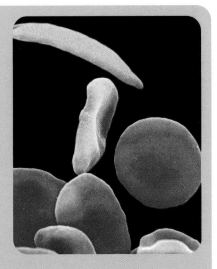

Above: *A normal red blood cell (rounded, right) and an elongated sickle-shaped red blood cell (top). Sickle-cell anemia is named after the affected red blood cells (RBCs). Abnormal hemoglobin distorts the RBCs into the sickle shape.*

CHAPTER FIVE

"{Mapping the human genome has made it} conceivable that our children's children will know the term cancer only as a constellation of stars." **PRESIDENT BILL CLINTON, 2000**

Genetics in Action

The story of the discovery of DNA did not end in 1953. Although its structure was revealed, many other mysteries about DNA remained. Genes differ by organism. The sequence, or order—and there are billions of combinations in which the nitrogenous base pairs appear—also differs by organism. Unraveling the shape of DNA was only the beginning. Scientists soon began to identify the different parts of the complex code of life.

Above: Deciphering the human genome was a huge project. Here, a scientist maps long DNA fragments on chromosomes. The chromosomes show on the monitor in red. DNA fragments appear in yellow.

THE HUMAN GENOME PROJECT (HGP)

A genome is the entire genetic map of an organism that contains all the biological information needed for life. In 1990, the United States Department of Energy and the National Institutes of Health began coordinating a worldwide effort to map the human genome. This huge project—the biological equivalent of putting a man on the Moon—cost $3 billion.

At least thirty thousand genes—with about three billion nitrogenous base pairs—carry the codes for proteins in human DNA. Scientists had to determine the order in which the bases (A, T, C, and G) appear on DNA in order to map the human genome. They believed that this massive task would take them about fifteen years to complete. Scientists finished the genome-mapping task much sooner than anticipated, thanks to advancements in computer technology. A complete version of the HGP—a genetic "blueprint" for human life—was published in 2003, only fifty years after Watson and Crick identified the structure of DNA. One of the biggest surprises scientists encountered was that 97 percent of human DNA has no known purpose; it does not appear to code for anything. Researchers call this "junk DNA" (or "non-coding DNA") and hope to someday determine its function.

The HGP analyzed the pooled DNA of a number of anonymous male and female donors. The results apply to all of us; humans share 99.9 percent of their DNA. The 0.1 percent that differs is the part that makes each person an individual. These variations occur when the order of bases in the DNA sequence switch for some reason, as seen below:

Above: *Siblings share many genes, but small differences in their DNA sequence of base pairs create individuals with unique genomes.*

Below: *A sample of human DNA (in capsule) is held in front of a graph that maps a DNA base-pairing sequence. Researchers hope their ability to "read" DNA will lead to future discoveries in scientific and medical knowledge.*

A G C T C C G A
A G T T C C G A

Scientists refer to the points in our genes that carry these base-pair variations as Single Nucleotide Polymorphisms (SNPs). About three million SNPs exist in the human genome in countless combinations—which results in a world of unique human beings. Identifying SNPs in individuals may lead to a greater understanding of disease and other inherited characteristics.

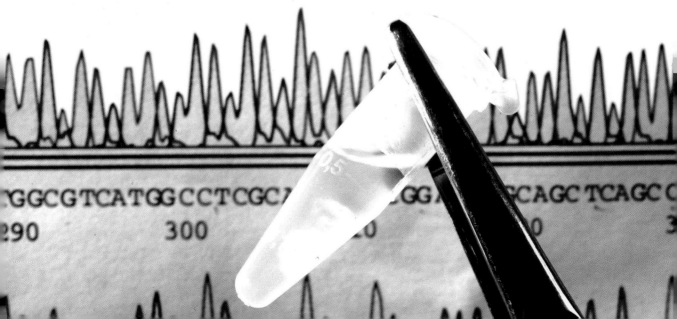

Fact

Fact

SWITCHING GENES
ON AND OFF
The newest stage
of gene research is
the international Human
Epigenome Project (HEP).
Launched in 2003, this
project seeks to identify
the factors that control
genes in the human body.
HEP scientists will
search the HGP blueprint
for genetic patterns
that might cause
diseases. Researchers
hope to discover exactly
what turns genes on and
off to make cells healthy
or diseased.

Below: Mitochondrial DNA (mtDNA).
Although mtDNA contains the same
nucleotide bases (adenine, cytosine,
guanine, thymine) as other human
DNA, it has a circular—rather than
helical—shape.

The mapping of the human genome is an important accomplishment in the development of genetics in the twenty-first century. Scientists hope that this knowledge about variations among individuals leads to revolutionary new ways to diagnose, treat, and—perhaps someday—prevent disease.

DNA: A KEY TO THE PAST

Advances in DNA technology not only tell us about our genes today, but also provide us with information about the genes of our ancestors.

DNA is a mixture of the genetic material inherited from one's parents. We cannot accurately determine which genes came from which parent at fertilization. Present technology can trace only two sources of DNA: The Y chromosome carries genes only between father and son. Females pass along their mitochondrial DNA (mtDNA) to offspring of either sex, but only subsequent generations of females carry that line of mtDNA; it remains unaffected by the male genes. Geneticists study the patterns of DNA inheritance using the Y chromosome and mtDNA, to make discoveries about our pasts that would have been impossible from normal

historical records. This branch of science—called population genetics—often reveals extraordinary facts.

Population geneticists study well-documented ancestry records to trace centuries of human history. For example, the Jewish priesthood tradition began about three thousand years ago, when Moses appointed his brother, Aaron, as the first high priest—a position that always passes from father to son. All members of the Jewish priesthood, called the Cohanim, therefore descended from Aaron. Chromosomal analyses of the Cohanim show that a very high percentage of them share a particular Y chromosome sequence, suggesting that they are, indeed, descended from one man.

Historical documents suggest that the actions of Spanish conquistadores (conquerors/invaders) who arrived in South America in the sixteenth century had devastating effects upon the local population; genetic evidence now proves that these accounts were no exaggeration. In Colombia, a study of mtDNA and Y-chromosome information reveals that mtDNA is more "Amerindian," while the Y chromosome is more "European." This study suggests that the invading

Above: When Spanish invaders conquered parts of South America in the sixteenth century, they killed most of the men, took the women as their wives, and produced many offspring. Tests on mtDNA and Y chromosomes reveal that many inhabitants of these areas are descendants of South American women and European men.

Fact

MITOCHONDRIAL DNA (mtDNA)
Mitochondria are rod-shaped bodies found in the cytoplasm of most cells. Chemical reactions in the mitochondria produce the energy for other chemical reactions within the cell. Mitochondria have their own DNA, called mtDNA. Sperm do not carry mtDNA; only eggs do. When a fertilized egg develops into an embryo, every cell contains mtDNA that is directly inherited from the mother. Any mutations in mtDNA pass to offspring via the female parent. Mitochondrial DNA exists long after a person's death. It can be extracted from bodies years later for testing.

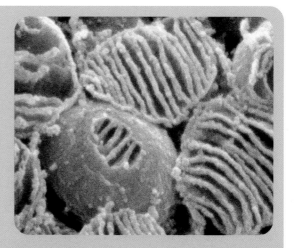

Above: Mitochondria magnified fifty thousand times actual size. They are the powerhouses of cells. Mitochondrial DNA (mtDNA) passes to subsequent generations via the female lineage.

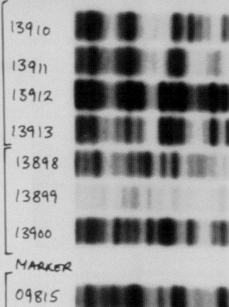

Fact

GENEALOGY

Genealogy (from the Latin word, "genus," meaning "race," or "family," and the Greek word, "logos," meaning "the study of") is the study of family origins and history. For many centuries, people traced their ancestry using written documents such as church and civic records. Modern DNA technology enables scientists to expand this field of study into a fascinating new branch, called population genetics.

Spaniards, who took the native women as "brides," basically wiped out the native male population.

Population genetics also allows anthropologists to follow global migrations of humans, tracking the changes and similarities in their genetic makeup. The long arm of population genetics even stretches back to the dawn of human origins: Current research focuses on the evolution of the human race in Africa and its subsequent migration to all the continents.

DNA "FINGERPRINTS"

Just as the police use ordinary fingerprints to establish the identity of a person who was present at the scene of a crime, so geneticists can identify people from a small sample of genetic material. DNA from the hair, skin, nail, blood, or other bodily fluids and tissues from one person all have the same DNA "fingerprint."

In 1984, British geneticist Alec Jeffreys (b. 1950) discovered that a small number of non-coding ("junk") genes contain repetitive stretches of DNA. Jeffreys realized that the number and length of the repetitions varies between people. He developed a technique that enabled him to identify people using small samples of their DNA. His method creates a photograph that looks like a bar code, or UPC (Universal Product Code) symbol. If the bar codes from two different samples match, then those tissue samples very likely came from the same person.

Still, DNA testing—sometimes called DNA fingerprinting—is not foolproof: It is only effective if samples are properly collected and free from contamination. Ongoing research and advancements in quality control for genetic sampling and analyses help ensure the accuracy of DNA testing techniques to more than 99.9 percent in nearly all cases. Even so, errors still occur, even with proper techniques. For this reason, DNA testing is often used along with other criminal evidence to suggest a person's guilt.

Fact

THE USES OF DNA TESTING

★ Forensic scientists can match the DNA of a tissue sample left at a crime scene with that of a possible suspect. It cannot prove a person's guilt, but it can provide a very strong probability of guilt. The chances of two humans (other than identical twins) having the same genetic makeup are miniscule. DNA testing can only prove someone's innocence —if the two samples are different, the suspect cannot be guilty.

★ DNA testing is used in paternity testing to prove whether or not people are related. In one controversial case, DNA tests revealed that Thomas Jefferson, third president of the United States, fathered at least one of the children of his slave, Sally Hemmings.

★ DNA testing of tissues from a dead body or skeletal remains can identify a person years, or even centuries, after death.

★ Population geneticists study DNA profiles to track the movement of peoples across continents and around the world.

Above: Nearly two centuries after his death, DNA testing revealed that Thomas Jefferson fathered at least one child with Sally Hemmings, one of his slaves.

GENETIC ENGINEERING

As scientists learned more about DNA, they also discovered ways to change the genetic structure of animals and plants. This new scientific field, called "genetic engineering," may change human history.

The DNA of plants and animals is remarkably similar, which means that scientists can sometimes splice together, or combine, genes of different species. In 1972, biochemist Paul Berg (b. 1926) spliced together genes to create a new form of DNA called "recombinant DNA." In 2000, researcher Ingo Potrykus (b. 1933) introduced daffodil genes into rice using recombinant DNA techniques. The new rice carries genes that produce beta-carotene, a chemical that our bodies turn into Vitamin A. Potrykus's new rice was yellow, so he named it "Golden Rice." In poor countries, about two million children die every year from Vitamin A deficiencies and about half a million others go blind. Golden Rice holds the promise of

Above: Arabidopsis thaliana, *or thale cress, a little-known weed of no commercial interest, became the first flowering plant to divulge the secrets of its DNA code. In 1996, a worldwide collaboration between geneticists began sequencing the genes of this plant. By the end of 1999, the project was complete—but although scientists learned the sequence of genes on each of the plant's five chromosomes, they do not know how each gene contributes to the life of the plant.*

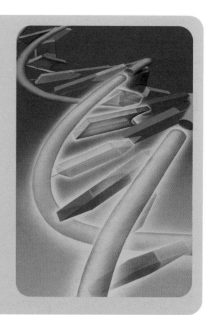

Fact

RECOMBINANT DNA

Gene splicing uses a type of circular DNA, called a plasmid, from a bacterium. A "useful" gene from some other organism is inserted into the plasmid, which is reinserted into the bacterium. The plasmid now contains newly created DNA, called recombinant DNA. After the bacterium reproduces—or clones—itself millions of times, it is injected into the "target" organism, which incorporates the recombinant DNA into its own genotype. Genes for desired characteristics can thus transfer to another—often completely different—species.

Right: Recombinant DNA techniques transfer a recombined, desired gene sequence (pink "backbone") to an original strand of DNA (greenish-blue "backbone").

Key People

Herbert Boyer (b. 1936) and **Stanley Cohen** (b. 1922) are American biochemists who began working together in 1972. In 1973, they combined their research on enzymes and plasmids to pioneer the techniques used in genetic engineering. They introduced specific DNA fragments into bacterial plasmids and made copies (clones) of the bacteria. Boyer and Cohen are considered the founding fathers of genetic engineering.

someday changing these outcomes. Developing a new strain of rice seeds in the laboratory, however, is a long way from sowing those seeds in paddies around the world—and even further away from tackling the poverty, ending political unrest, or solving the other causes leading to malnutrition.

GENETIC MODIFICATION

When bacteria reproduce, they make identical copies of themselves. Genetic modification (GM) techniques use these exact copies, or clones, by inserting them into other organisms. Much current research is devoted to developing, improving, and cultivating GM crops. For example, certain plants that produce large amounts of oil in their seeds could possibly help us reduce our dependence on fossil fuels for energy production. Other plants naturally break down toxic materials (pollutants or poisons) in the water or soil. Scientists are looking at ways to use GM to incorporate the gene sequence for cleaning up toxics into plants that are easy to cultivate. Another major area of GM research centers on increasing food crop resistance to disease. This could reduce the world's dependence upon chemical fertilizers and pesticides.

Scientists compare using GM to the selective breeding of plants and animals employed by farmers for thousands of years. The crucial difference is that traditional breeding methods do not introduce genes from other species. Scientists cannot predict the long-term effects of GM organisms on the ecosystem; this, together with other ethical factors, causes much concern in many countries.

Experience shows the need for extensive testing of new technologies. Far too often, new technologies or procedures that seem like miraculous solutions to problems quickly create even bigger problems.

CLONING

In 1996, geneticists used a technique called Somatic Cell Nuclear Transfer to reach a milestone in their

Above: GM tomatoes have a longer shelf life than non-modified tomatoes.

Below: Genetic engineering techniques produce crops with altered DNA, giving them beneficial properties, such as increased resistance to weed killer. This researcher is comparing the growth of GM sugar beet plants with that of natural sugar beet plants.

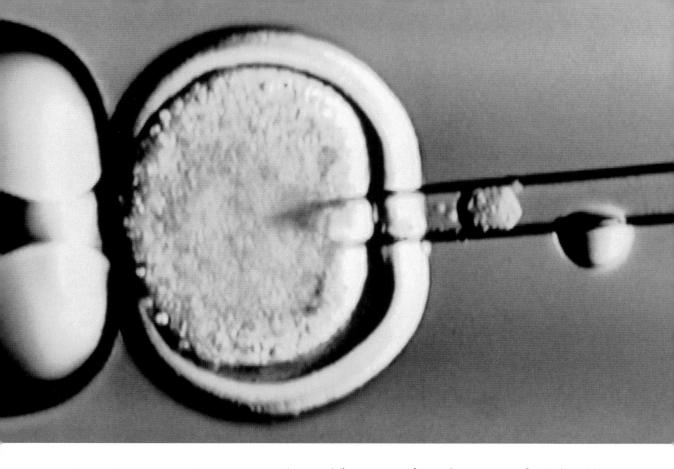

Above: *After removal of the original genetic material from a sheep's egg cell, the new DNA being injected will control the cell's growth and functions.*

Below: *Dolly the sheep died in 2003 from a lung ailment and severe arthritis at the relatively young age of six. Her necropsy revealed that, other than the lung problem and arthritis, she had developed normally.*

science: They created a sheep named Dolly. The geneticists replaced the nucleus from an adult sheep's egg cell with the nucleus of one of her non-sex, body (or "somatic") cells. Next, the researchers planted the egg with the switched nucleus into the mother sheep's uterus, where it developed into a fetus without being fertilized by sperm. Dolly, the cloned baby lamb born from this procedure, had exactly the same DNA as her mother. This method of generating an animal with identical DNA is called "reproductive cloning." Cloned animals tend to suffer high rates of deformity, disability, premature aging, and early death.

The cells in a fertilized egg divide and multiply until they form a ball of cells called a blastocyst. This contains stem cells—undifferentiated cells with the potential to develop into any kind of body cell, such as a nerve cell, a kidney cell, or a muscle cell. In this way, stem cells are like basic building materials for living organisms. Stem-cell researchers hope to control exactly what type of tissue develops from stem cells and then use them to grow tissues or entire organs for use in transplants, to help cure diseases, and to treat

Left: Many diabetics, like this young boy, must inject themselves with insulin—a hormone normally made in the pancreas. Insulin helps the body use blood sugar for energy. Diabetics do not create enough insulin. Stem-cell research may one day lead to better treatments, or even cures, for diseases such as diabetes.

certain disabilities. Many people object to stem-cell research, citing religious, moral, and ethical grounds.

The governments of some countries sponsor a type of stem-cell research—called therapeutic cloning—that uses DNA from discarded human embryos or embryos created specifically for research purposes. In 2001, the U.S. government outlawed the use of federal money for stem-cell research on cells removed from discarded embryos, but continued funding research on embryonic cell lines that already existed when the law was passed. Privately funded stem-cell research on newer cell lines continues in the United States.

In February 2004, scientists at Seoul University in Korea announced a breakthrough in therapeutic cloning: They created the most advanced human embryo clones to date using thirty blastocysts created from DNA provided by volunteers. Each blastocyst eventually developed into specific cell types, such as blood or bone. This research is expected to lead to treatments for disorders such as diabetes, arthritis, Alzheimer's, and Parkinson's disease. Scientists and doctors hope to transplant tissues generated from such stem-cell research into patients with these ailments.

Despite objections to the use of human embryos, therapeutic cloning techniques may someday improve the outlook on life for millions of people with inherited diseases and may give hope to millions more who suffer from disabilities caused by accidents.

Fact

CLONING ENDANGERED SPECIES
Scientists hope to someday use reproductive cloning techniques to generate new populations of endangered animal species. In 2001, Italian scientists reported that they had successfully cloned a mouflon—an endangered species of wild sheep. The cloned mouflon now lives in a wildlife park on the Italian island of Sardinia. No one knows if the mouflon, like Dolly the sheep, will develop illnesses as a result of the cloning. Other potential candidates for cloning include the Sumatran tiger and the giant panda.

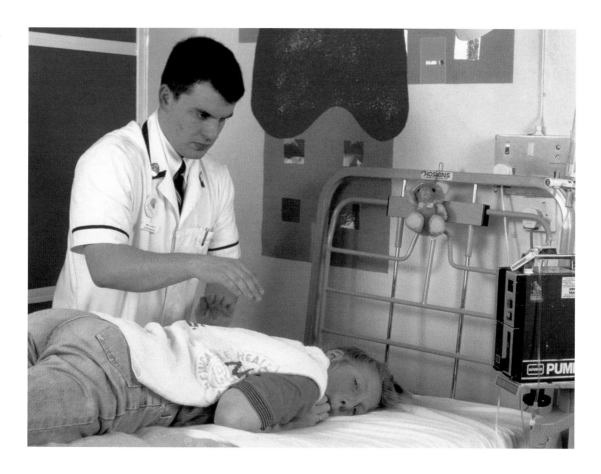

Above: People suffering from cystic fibrosis need daily respiratory therapy to help loosen the mucus that obstructs their lungs. Medical researchers hope to develop a gene therapy that may alleviate some of the problems caused by this disease.

GENE THERAPY

Cystic fibrosis (CF) is an inherited disease that affects the lungs and other tissues. People with CF produce a thick mucus that clogs their lungs and makes them prone to infection. If a child inherits a copy of the CF gene from both parents, he or she will develop this life-threatening disease. Gene therapy for CF works by replacing faulty genes in respiratory cells with cells of normal respiratory cells. Nose drops, or a tube, deliver the normal genes directly to the sufferer's airways. The new genes instruct the respiratory tissues to produce a more watery mucus, like normal lung cells. The treatment is not a permanent cure. It does not change the person's genotype, and the sufferer can still pass the CF gene on to his or her own children—but it is a giant leap forward in treating this debilitating illness.

Although CF gene therapy is in its experimental phase, such successes prove that gene replacement therapy may someday come into play against other inherited conditions. One of the many problems of incorporating new genes into cells is that viruses are often used to transport the DNA. These viruses may cause the recipient's immune system to create antibodies, which then fight the virus. Extreme reactions to the gene therapy may even cause cancer. To overcome these problems, U.S. researchers created a compact form of DNA that is so tiny it can pass directly through a cell membrane without using a transporting virus.

Gene therapy can also indirectly lessen the symptoms of faulty genes. For example, transfusions of the clotting substance Factor VIII (Factor Eight), isolated from sheeps' milk, helps ease the problems associated with hemophilia, a human disease caused by an inherited blood protein abnormality. Hemophiliacs—people who lack the protein that makes blood clot—can bleed to death from even a small cut. Factor VIII used to be obtained only from donated human blood. Gene therapy techniques created sheep that produce Factor VIII in their milk—reducing the risk of contracting diseases from donated human blood products.

Fact

THE RISKS OF GENE THERAPY
Jesse Gelsinger, an eighteen-year-old who suffered from an inherited liver disorder, died in September 1999 after participating in a gene-therapy research trial. Jesse had hoped that, while the experiment would not cure him, it might offer hope to babies born with his disease. Jesse's major organs failed soon after he received a virus that carried the corrective genes into his body. He probably died from a reaction to the virus that carried the genes.

Left: Blood centers use donated blood in a number of ways. Some blood units are used for whole-blood transfusions, while other units are separated into different blood components, such as blood serum, packed red blood cells, platelets, or Factor VIII clotting substance. Although medical facilities will always require a fresh supply of blood, genetic engineering techniques allow scientists to develop other methods of supplying some cultivated blood products—and with less risk of contamination for patients.

CHAPTER SIX

"You might decide to remove a gene because it increases the risk of something bad, and only later realize that it was protecting you against something else that was bad."

HUGH WATKINS, WELLCOME TRUST CENTRE FOR HUMAN GENETICS, 2003

The Road Ahead

"Genetic engineering" is a broad term that covers all the techniques used by researchers to manipulate the genome of an organism. As advances in genetic techniques occur, we face the prospect of making decisions that will affect the evolution of our species and that of the other organisms with which we share our planet. Such decisions deserve serious consideration and must be undertaken with the understanding that all of us—not just the scientists—must share the responsibility of making proper choices now and for the future.

Above: Many people fear that genetic engineering will have detrimental effects on humans. How will we react if scientists can one day clone human beings or produce a generation of genetically perfect babies?

ETHICAL DILEMMAS

Advances in genetics pose ethical dilemmas for society. When Charles Darwin suggested that some individuals have desirable characteristics, a few people argued that society should encourage those individuals to breed, while discouraging others with less-than-desirable characteristics to remain child-free. This theory, known as eugenics—the science of being well-born—was popular at the beginning of the twentieth century. Many people looked at eugenics as a way of improving the human gene pool by weeding out inferior traits. In the 1930s, the National Socialist Workers' Party (the Nazi Party) in Germany ordered the compulsory sterilization or extermination (killing) of people with mental disabilities. Other target groups included people with physical disabilities, Jews, gypsies, and homosexuals. The Nazi eugenics policy killed millions of innocent people.

Modern genetics survives in the shadow of eugenics: Scientists recognize that we must not repeat past mistakes. Still, some fear that knowledge of a person's DNA profile could somehow be used to discriminate against those with "faulty" genes. Could insurance companies, for instance, cite a person's genetic makeup and refuse to provide medical coverage for a client whose genes indicate a strong possibility of developing a life-threatening disease? Could insurance companies also deny that person life insurance?

Genetic screening makes it possible to learn if an unborn child carries certain genetic defects. For example, Tay-Sachs disease is a genetic nerve-cell disorder that often passes to offspring if both parents carry the Tay-Sachs gene. Tay-Sachs sufferers seldom live past age five. DNA testing can help such couples know in advance if they must prepare for caring for a child with extreme health problems. Such information presents parents with very difficult situations.

Below: Amniocentesis is a prenatal (before birth) procedure involving the extraction a small amount of amniotic fluid (the liquid that cushions and protects the developing fetus). Prenatal tests can reveal genetic disorders in a developing fetus.

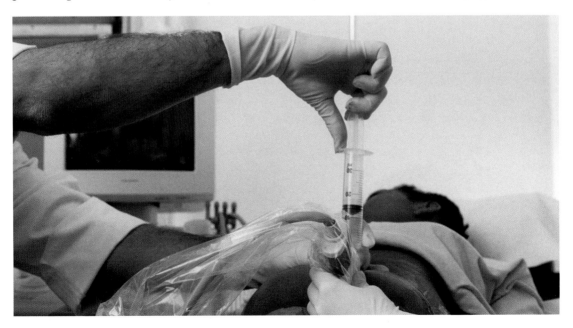

Above: People and governments often disagree about the safety of GM food crops. While the European Union supports the idea of labeling all GM food, the United States, Canada, and Argentina believe that only foods with significant genetic alterations need GM labeling. Other countries, such as Australia, Japan, and New Zealand are currently studying the GM-labeling issue.

Genetic screening may one day predict the likelihood of someone contracting a particular illness. People could use results from genetic screening tests to change their diets and lifestyles to help avoid—or at least lessen—the effects of a disease or condition they are prone to develop. Would you want to know if your genes were likely to someday trigger an inherited disease, certain cancers, or heart ailments?

THE ECONOMICS OF GENETIC RESEARCH

Genetic engineering is not just about preventing and curing diseases or growing bigger and better crops; genetic engineering is also good business. Companies behind the research and development of GM agriculture techniques stand to reap large profits from their discoveries. Medical research and pharmaceutical companies, also lured by future economic benefits, are racing to explore an enormous range of applications and procedures that incorporate genetic engineering techniques. Their research opens new frontiers of knowledge in the health sciences industry—frontiers that promise advanced treatments, or even cures, for devastating diseases. Chances are, new technologies developed as a result of genetic engineering research will someday become part of our everyday lives in ways that are impossible to imagine right now.

Key People

Francis Galton (1822–1911) was a cousin of Charles Darwin and a pioneer of eugenics. He favored the selective breeding of humans as a way to improve Britain's genetic stock. Galton believed that people of lower intelligence should not have children. His ideas were popular for a time but never became established—although they unwittingly gave rise to groups such as the Nazi Party in the 1930s. the Nazis believed in creating a "superior Aryan race." Though Galton's ideas regarding eugenics are unacceptable, he made many other contributions to science, including the idea that everyone's fingerprints are unique.

THE FUTURE OF DNA RESEARCH

Just over fifty years ago, the discovery of DNA marked the beginning of a new era in science. Thanks to Watson and Crick's discovery, we can now tell if our unborn children are healthy. We can lessen the effects of some life-threatening diseases. We can convict criminals with nearly perfect certainty while freeing those wrongly accused. Many of our food crops are grown with disease-resistant seeds, and other GM crops last longer on grocery store shelves without spoiling. No matter where else DNA research leads, it will continue to touch countless lives into the future.

Below: As research into genetics continues, we must ask ourselves how to best deal with the possibilities it presents to us.

"It is fairly certain that some GM foods will cause problems. Low risk is not no risk. The question is one which is universal in economics—will the benefits outweigh the costs?"

STEVE JONES, BRITISH GENETICIST

TIME LINE

1735	Carl Linnaeus proposes a taxonomic system based on shared characteristics for the naming of organisms
1798	Thomas Malthus publishes his essay on populations and their struggle for existence
1809	Jean Baptiste Lamarck puts forward his ideas on evolution
1830	Charles Lyell publishes his book on geology and suggests the Earth is much older than previously thought
1831	Charles Darwin sets out on his epic voyage on HMS *Beagle*; nuclei are identified within cells
1839	Cell theory—all organisms are made of cells—is developed
1859	Charles Darwin publishes *On the Origin of Species by Process of Natural Selection*
1865	Gregor Mendel publishes his finding on the principles of heredity
1868	Johann Friedrich Miescher isolates nucleic acid (later known as DNA)
1879	Walther Flemming describes chromosomes during cell division
1887	August Weismann observes that sex cells have half the number of chromosomes
1899	The first International Congress of Genetics is held in London
1900	Hugo de Vries discovers Mendel's work
1905	William Bateson names the new branch of science "genetics"
1910	Thomas Hunt Morgan discovers gene-linked traits through his work with fruit flies
1929	Phoebus Levene discovers deoxyribose sugars in nucleic acids
1944	Oswald Avery describes DNA as the genetic material
1950	Edwin Chargaff shows that the numbers of bases in DNA exist in a strict pattern: adenosine pairs with thymine and guanine pairs with cytosine
1953	Using X-ray crystallography completed by Rosalind Franklin and Maurice Wilkins, James Watson and Francis Crick discover and describe the double-helix structure of DNA
1967	Amniocentesis, a technique used to identify genetic abnormalities in unborn children, is used for the first time
1972	Paul Berg produces the first recombinant DNA
1973	Herbert Boyer and Stanley Cohen pioneer genetic engineering
1984	Alec Jeffreys develops genetic fingerprinting
1990	The Human Genome Project begins
1994	Genetically modified tomatoes go on sale for the first time
1996	Dolly the (cloned) sheep is born
2003	The results from the Human Genome Project are published; Dolly the sheep is euthanized

GLOSSARY

adaptation the ability of an organism to change to survive in its environment.

adenine one of the four nitrogenous bases of DNA; always pairs with thymine.

amino acid a building block of proteins.

anthropologists people who study the development of human beings.

antibodies blood proteins that help fight off infections, viruses, and diseases.

bacteria (singular: bacterium) single-celled organisms with no distinct nucleus and single-stranded DNA.

blastocyst a rounded cluster of cells that forms early in the development of an embryo.

Chargaff's rule the principle that the numbers of complementary DNA bases are always equal.

chromosome a rod-like structure within the cell's nucleus; contains genetic material (DNA).

clone an individual produced without sexual reproduction; it contains DNA identical to its parent organism.

cytosine one of the four nitrogenous bases of DNA; always pairs with guanine.

DNA deoxyribonucleic acid: a molecule with a double-helix structure, found in chromosomes. DNA carries the genetic code for organisms.

double helix a structure that resembles a spiral staircase.

enzymes natural body chemicals that act as catalysts to initiate cell reactions.

ethics a set of social rules that govern proper actions, reactions, and behavior.

evolution the theory that organisms undergo slow changes over time that help them best exist in their environment.

fertilization the joining of male and female sex cells, which results in a new organism with a complete set of chromosomes.

forensic the scientific examination and analysis of physical material that holds clues, such as what caused the death of organic matter.

fossil the impression of or remains of an animal or plant preserved within rock.

gene the basic unit of heredity, found on chromosomes, that transmits information from one cell generation to the next.

genetic engineering the manipulation of an organism's genetic material to cause changes.

generation a group of individuals separate from its parents.

genome the entire set of genetic material DNA found in the nucleus and mitochondria.

genotype an organism's genetic identity.

germ cells (gametes) sex cells, such as sperm, pollen, and ova, that contain half the normal number of chromosomes.

guanine one of the four nitrogenous bases of DNA; always pairs with cytosine.

helix a loosely coiled spiral structure.

hemoglobin a blood protein that carries oxygen around the body.

hemophilia a disease that interferes with the blood's normal ability to form clots.

hemophiliacs people affected with the disease known as hemophilia.

heredity the genetic qualities passed from ancestor to offspring.

hybrid the organism that results from the mixing of two different types of organisms; may show blended characteristics of each parent in that or subsequent generations.

hypothesis an educated guess.

inheritance the genetic qualities received from preceeding generations.

junk DNA DNA with no apparent function; also called non-coding DNA.

malnutrition a condition resulting from a diet lacking the essential components necessary to produce and sustain a healthy organism.

morals a set of rules that defines right or wrong actions and/or behaviors of a group.

meiosis cell division that forms sex cells, each with a single set of chromosomes, rather than the double set found in other body cells.

mitochondria cell organelles that provide energy for all cell functions; contain strands of DNA passed to offspring through the mother.

mitosis cell division that results in two identical cells with complete sets of chromosomes.

mRNA messenger RNA; carries information from nuclear DNA to the cytoplasmic ribosomes, which then create new proteins.

mtDNA mitochondrial DNA; passed to offspring through female parent.

mutations random changes in an organism's genetic material.

natural selection the slow process by which generations of organisms undergo genetic changes over time that help them adapt to and survive in their environment.

necropsy the examination of an animal's body after death.

nucleotide a genetic unit formed from a sugar molecule, a nitrogenous base and a phosphate; chains of nucleotides form DNA strands.

paternity relating to the father.

phenotype an organism's physical appearance; determined by its genotype and environment.

protein molecules made from amino acids that help direct a cell's form and function.

reproductive cloning production of a living copy of an organism; formed by substituting the DNA from an egg with the DNA of a somatic cell, so that the copy (clone) has the same genotype as its mother.

ribosome cell organelles that synthesize, or produce, proteins.

RNA ribonucleic acid; transmits information from DNA to manufacture proteins in the cytoplasm.

siblings children with one common parent.

SNP Single Nucleotide Polymorphisms: variations in genetic code; can cause mutations.

species a group of animals or plants that can breed with one another and produce fertile offspring.

stem cells new, undifferentiated cells that can grow into many different types of tissue, such as nerves, bone, or liver tissue.

therapeutic cloning the creation of healthy human cells to experiment upon or to cultivate as replacement cells to cure specific conditions.

thymine one of the four nitrogenous bases of DNA; always pairs with adenine.

tRNA transfer RNA; a molecule that bonds with amino acids and transfers them to ribosomes, where proteins are made.

undifferentiated cells stem cells that have the potential to develop into any type of cells.

uracil one of the four nitrogenous bases of RNA; always pairs with adenine.

virus a primitive organism that consists of genetic material surrounded by a protein casing; it can only reproduce when inside another organism.

X chromosome one of the two sex chromosomes. The ovum only carries an X chromosome. An ovum fertilized with a sperm cell carrying an X chromosome produces a female offspring.

Y chromosome one of the two sex chromosomes. Sperm cells carry either an X or a Y chromosome. An ovum fertilized with a sperm cell carrying a Y chromosome produces a male offspring.

FURTHER INFORMATION

BOOKS

Cefrey, Holly. *Cloning and Genetic Engineering. High Interest Books* (series).
  Children's Press (2002).

Discovery Channel School Science *Genetics. Universes Large and Small* (series).
  Gareth Stevens Publishing (2004).

Dowswell, Paul. *Genetic Engineering. 21st Century Issues* (series). Gareth Stevens Publishing (2004).

Fritz, Sandy. *Genomics and Cloning. Hot Science* (series). Smart Apple Media (2003).

Fridell, Ron. *DNA Fingerprinting: The Ultimate Identity.* Franklin Watts (2001).

Graham, Ian. *Genetics: The Study of Heredity. Investigating Science* (series).
  Gareth Stevens Publishing (2002).

Kowalski, Kathiann M. *The Debate Over Genetically Engineered Foods: Healthy or Harmful?*
  Issues in Focus (series). Enslow (2002).

Parker, Steve. *Genetic Engineering. Face the Facts* (series). Raintree (2005).

WEB SITES

http://ology.amnh.org/genetics/index.html
Take a genetic journey through the Gene Scene.

www.yourgenome.org
Choose your interest level as you investigate the latest news and research on genetics.

www.doegenomes.org
Discover the United States Department of Energy research on the Human Genome Project.

http://gslc.genetics.utah.edu/
Explore the diverse links on this site for interactive tours on genetic topics.

www.genecrc.org/site/ko/index_ko.htm
Play some genetic games while you learn about genes and DNA.

www.thetech.org/genetics/
Learn what color eyes your children will have as you explore the many links on this site.

www.dnaftb.org/dnaftb/
Visit all three animated sections for information about DNA, genes, and heredity.

INDEX